Indian Nations

THE ONEIDA

by
L. Gordon McLester III and Elisabeth G. Torres

General Editors
Herman J. Viola and David Jeffery

A Rivilo Book

**RAINTREE
STECK-VAUGHN
PUBLISHERS**
RSVP®

A Harcourt Company

Austin · New York
www.steck-vaughn.com

Special thanks to my family, the Oneida Elders,
Gerald L. Hill, and Judy Cornelius for their support and help.
—Gordon McLester

Published by Raintree Steck-Vaughn Company, an imprint of the
Steck-Vaughn Company

Developed for Steck-Vaughn Company by Rivilo Books
Editor: David Jeffery
Photo Research: Brenda McLain
Design: Barbara Lisenby and Todd Hirshman
Electronic Preparation: Lyda Guz

Raintree Steck-Vaughn Publishers Staff
Publishing Director: Walter Kossmann
Editor: Kathy DeVico

Photo Credits: Charles Leonard: cover, pp. 18, 21, 26 left and bottom right, 27, 28 left, 30 bottom, 32 left and center, 34, 36, 43; Lisa Ranallo Horse Capture: pp. 4, 6; Alan and Sandy Carey/Photodisc: p. 7; John Kahionhes Fadden: pp. 8, 14, 24; National Anthropological Archives/Smithsonian Institution: pp. 9, 15 top, 25 bottom, 26 top right, 31; Tomasz Tomaszewski/National Geographic Society Image Collection: p. 10 right; Corbis: p. 10 left, 16; Peter Chen/Syracuse Newspapers: p. 11; Hamilton College, New York: pp. 12, 13; Richard Walker/New York State Historical Association: p. 15 bottom; L. Gordon McLester: pp. 22, 35 right, 38; Kalihwisaks Newspaper: pp. 23, 39; Bobbi Webster: p. 25 top; Melissa Mahan/Democrat and Chronicle: p. 28 right; Michelle Gabel/Syracuse Newspapers: p. 29; Mary Lemieux: p. 30 top; National Museum of Natural History/Smithsonian Institution: p. 32 right; Bettmann/Corbis: pp. 35 left, 40 top; New York Public Library: p. 37; Associated Press/Empire Expo Center: p. 40 bottom; Lyda Guz: p. 42.

Library of Congress Cataloging-in-Publication Data
McLester, L. Gordon.
    The Oneida / by L. Gordon McLester III and Elisabeth G. Torres.
        p. cm. — (Indian nations)
    Includes bibliographical references and index.
    ISBN 0-8172-5457-9
    1. Oneida Indians — History — Juvenile literature.   2. Oneida Indians — Social life and customs — Juvenile literature. [1. Oneida Indians. 2. Indians of North America — New York (State). 3. Indians of North America — Ontario.]
    I. Torres, Elisabeth G. II. Title. III. Indian nations (Austin, Tex.)
    E99.O45 .M35 2001
    974.7004'9755—dc21

                                   00-034162

Printed and bound in the United States
1 2 3 4 5 6 7 8 9 0 LB 04 03 02 01 00

Cover photo: Huston V. Wheelock, a veteran of the Korean War,
is dressed for his role as a traditional Oneida dancer.

Contents

Creation Story

The Oneida people share a **legend** with the other five **nations** of the Iroquois Confederation about the origins of "Mother Earth." The story begins long ago when there was no Earth as we know it today, but only a Sky World filled with beings called Sky People. The Sky People lived on the bounty provided by a heavenly tree. It had beautiful white blossoms that gave off light. The tree also had long branches that covered the Sky World and provided food for everyone.

One day a young Sky Woman who was expecting a child decided to dig at the roots of the **Great Tree**. She thought that she would gather and cook some of its roots. While digging she discovered an opening into another world. The Sky Woman was very curious and began leaning into the hole to get a better look. When she did this, she slipped and fell headfirst into the hole. As she fell, she grabbed at the roots of the Great Tree, which broke off and fell with her into the world of water beneath.

As Sky Woman fell, she cried out for help. She was heard by the birds and other creatures. Great white swans lowered her carefully down to the water, where a giant sea turtle allowed her to be placed safely on its back. To help Sky Woman, a beaver dived into the water to locate mud to make dry land. But before he could return to the surface, he drowned. Sky Woman picked up the tiny creature and breathed into his mouth, and he came back to life.

◄ *Sky Woman fell from a hole in the sky, with roots of the Great Tree in her hand. Great swans caught her and lowered her to the back of a giant sea turtle.*

It was Muskrat who was finally able to bring to the surface a small clump of mud clutched in his tiny paws. Sky Woman placed the clump of mud on the back of the giant sea turtle. Then, as she walked in a circular motion on the turtle's back, the mud beneath her feet began to expand. It grew and grew until it became Mother Earth, the planet we live on today.

Sky Woman gave birth to a daughter, and her daughter gave birth to twin boys. One of the boys was born in the normal way and was good. The other was born pushing his way through his mother's side—killing her—and he was evil.

The Good Twin and the Evil Twin grew to become men. The Good Twin began to create good things like useful plants, animals, and clear-running streams. But the Evil Twin tried to ruin his brother's brilliant work. He created poisonous plants and diseases; he placed boulders in the streams and rivers.

The twins finally fought to see who was more powerful. The Good Twin won, but then the brothers realized that both good and evil are important on the Earth. The Good Twin then created human beings to enjoy all the wonderful things that he had made for them.

Folktale

Many stories were passed along by Oneida parents to their children. Here is one of them—the story about what a smart fox did to get the cheese he wanted.

The Fox and the Mice

Two mice had one piece of cheese, and they got into an argument about how to divide it. Both mice wanted equal parts. A fox came walking by. He was a great talker and told the mice that he would divide the cheese. The mice agreed. The fox started by dividing the cheese in two parts. But the first mouse said that his part was smaller. So the fox took a bite from the piece of cheese the second mouse had. The second mouse then said that now his piece was smaller than the one the first mouse had. So the fox took a bite from the piece of the first mouse. The fox went back and forth, taking more bites from the cheese each mouse had. When the fox had eaten all of their cheese, he said: "Now you are even, you both have nothing." The moral of the story is that you should learn to share or you'll wind up with nothing.

The fox is sly and cunning. In the story of the mice and the cheese, he found a way to make the greedy mice give the cheese to him. How did he do it?

Key Historical Events

Creation of the Confederacy

One legend tells how the **Iroquois Confederacy** was first created, probably before 1500. A Huron Indian known as **"The Peacemaker"** heard about constant fighting among the Iroquois nations. Because he hated war, he vowed to stop the feuding. The Peacemaker visited each of the warring nations. He told them that the Creator had sent him to deliver a message of peace.

The Peacemaker then pulled a large tree from the ground, which left a gaping hole. He told the warriors of each nation to throw their weapons of war into the hole. He then replanted the tree, which he called the **"Tree of Peace."** Finally, the Peacemaker explained to them the Great Law by which each Iroquois nation should live. He told them that if they took one arrow alone it can easily be broken, but if they bound the arrows together, they would be unbreakable. He also told them that if any nation wished to follow the Great Law and the Great Peace the group should sit under the Tree of Peace and be of one mind and one heart with their brothers. The Tree of Peace symbolized their pact. The roots of the Tree of Peace spread in the four directions of north, east, south, and west to hold the tree strong against all storms.

An Iroquois (Mohawk) artist, John Fadden, drew a symbolic scene of the "Tree of Peace" whose roots cover a war club.

First Encounter with Europeans

In the language of the Oneida (oh-NIGH-duh) their name for themselves means "people of the standing stone." They are members of the Iroquois Confederacy, or **Haudenosaunee**, "people of the **longhouse**." The Confederacy, formed before 1500, is an alliance among Indian nations that joined together to stop warfare with one another and live in peace. The Iroquois Confederacy now consists of the Oneida, Mohawk, Onondaga, Cayuga, Seneca, and Tuscarora nations. Originally there were only five member nations. The Tuscaroras joined in the 1700s. People of the Iroquois Confederation nations shared ceremonies, traditions, styles of clothing, and similar dialects of language.

Europeans began to enter Iroquois territory early in the 16th century. In 1535 the French explorer Jacques Cartier sailed up the St. Lawrence River, looking for a route to China, which he

A French map drawn in 1673 shows many details of Iroquois country that are familiar today. This includes the Great Lakes, at left, the St. Lawrence River, and the port of Quebec.

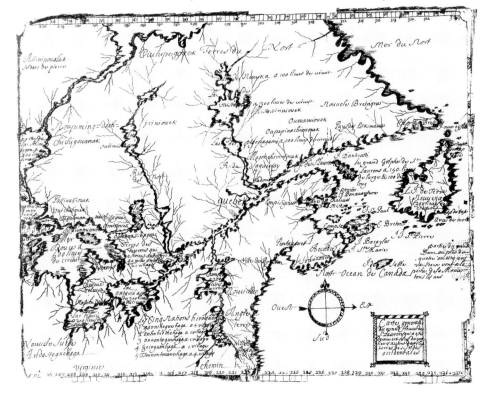

Explorer Samuel de Champlain (below) sailed westward past the Thousand Islands of the St. Lawrence River (right) in 1609. He met with members of the Iroquois Confederacy.

never found. Almost a hundred years passed before another European visited the Iroquois, the French explorer Samuel de Champlain, who arrived in 1609. Champlain dealt primarily with the Mohawks. Although the first meetings were not friendly, the French soon began trading with the Confederacy. The French exchanged glass beads, copper kettles, needles, weapons, and many other items that the Iroquois people desired. In exchange the French were given animal skins or pelts, usually those of beavers. Beaver skins were then very fashionable in Europe, where they were made into hats, coats, and other expensive garments. Other parts of the beaver were used for medicine, oils, and perfume.

The Dutch and Trading

French explorers and traders were soon followed by counterparts from the Netherlands, known as the Dutch. The Dutch and the Iroquois became very friendly with each other. In 1618 they made an agreement called the "Chain of Friendship," one that was later adopted by the British as well. The Dutch opened a trading post for the Iroquois called Fort Nassau near what is today Albany, New York. The fort lasted only two years because spring floods washed it away. However, because business with the Iroquois was so profitable, the Dutch immediately built another trading post a little farther away called Fort Orange. Not only did this post establish the Dutch as the Confederacy's

The Haudenosaunee (Iroquois) Standing Committee on Burial Rules and Regulations arranges artifacts returned to the people by the National Museum of the Smithsonian Institution, including wampum belts, strings, and beads.

primary trading partner, it also helped all the members of the Confederacy prosper because of the increase in trade goods.

An important Iroquois item of exchange was a woven belt made from wampum. Wampum was a tube-shaped bead made from the shells of clams. It came in two colors, purple and white. Some Indians who lived in the Northeast used wampum for ceremonial purposes. The Iroquois made belts using the wampum shells. About a foot long, Iroquois belts were not worn. Instead, they were used to record agreements made between nations. The Oneida used belts in the same way that Europeans used parchment or paper to record treaties. Overall, the Oneida and other Iroquois nations were quite hospitable toward Europeans. That was in keeping with their tradition of friendliness and hospitality to strangers.

Epidemics Ravage the Iroquois

Trading continued successfully until the summer of 1633. Then a fever carried by English settlers killed many English and Indians. The next year measles swept through the Iroquois' country. In 1634 another disease struck the Iroquois—smallpox, brought to them by the Dutch. Because Oneidas and other Iroquois peoples had never before been exposed to those illnesses, they had no natural immunity to them. As a result, hundreds of Oneidas died within a few years. Their population was cut in half.

Samuel Kirkland and Shenandoah

Samuel Kirkland

The next hundred years was a time of profound change for the Oneida as more and more white people moved into their country. The person who had, perhaps, the most influence on the nation was Samuel Kirkland. He was a Congregational clergyman who came in 1766 to establish a religious mission. At the mission, he taught the Oneida the English language, converted them to Christianity, and helped them abandon the use of whiskey, which they had first received from fur traders. When Kirkland arrived, there was strife in the community because the warriors felt they did not have enough power compared to the chiefs. Kirkland took advantage of the people's unhappiness and told them that following the Christian faith would save them.

However, the Oneida soon learned that Kirkland's ultimate goal was to rid them of their Indian culture and teach them to live the ways of the white people. This knowledge caused another uproar in the community, which now had followers of Christianity on the one hand and the old traditional religion on the other. Because Kirkland arrived during a very difficult time for the Oneida nation, his teachings seemed to offer salvation for the people and hope for a better future.

In 1999 at Hamilton College in New York, a memorial stone was added to the gravesite of the Oneida leader Shenandoah.

Samuel Kirkland was befriended by an Oneida leader, Shenandoah, who became a convert to Christianity. Although Shenandoah was older than Kirkland, the Oneida embraced the minister as a father figure. Shenandoah was born about 1706 to a Susquehanna Indian family. He was later adopted by the Oneida and eventually became an Oneida war chief. (Shenandoah means "the deer." His name is pronounced the same way as the river and song but is commonly spelled "Schenandoa" and various other ways.)

Seeds of Democracy

Some people in the English colonies eventually came to appreciate the importance of the Iroquois Confederacy. Many Iroquois ideas about democracy and freedom of expression even influenced political thinkers and writers in Europe. For example, it made no sense to the Oneida that the British were governed by kings and queens. Oneidas believed that no royal person could tell another person what to do or how to behave. For the Oneida, the people came first. Their chiefs gave suggestions, but they never commanded. The Oneida "counciled together" to make decisions.

An example of the Oneida's concern about people occurred after the Tuscarora Indian people of the Carolinas had fought against the taking of their land by the colonists. With their defeat and dispersal, the Tuscarora moved northward and found refuge with the Oneida in 1712. The Oneida also gave refuge to some displaced New England Indians, including the Brotherton and Stockbridge Indians, as they were called. No European nations were as generous with the displaced of their own continent.

The Tuscarora were adopted and given status as brothers with the Oneida and the Cayuga, another nation in the Iroquois Confederacy. The Tuscarora were given a right to sit in the **Grand Council** with the Oneida. Although the Tuscarora had no **sachems** (representatives) in Council, their voices were heard by means of the voices of Oneida sachems.

The American Revolution

The Oneidas, along with the other Iroquois nations, were troubled by the Revolutionary War. Begun in 1775, it pitted American colonists against the government of Great Britain. The war was largely fought over the principles of democracy. The colonists wanted to be free of British rule and of unfair taxes imposed by the British king and Parliament. The colonists also wanted the right to move west of the line along the Appalachian Mountains that was established by royal decree in 1763. The decree prohibited such movement. For their part, the British considered the American colonists to be selfish and ungrateful for all the services and protection the mother country had provided to its distant colonies.

As they had when their confederacy was established, Iroquois leaders met to consider peace in the 1770s.

Red Jacket was a reluctant supporter of the British during the American Revolution. After the war he was a principal spokesman for his people, the Seneca.

The Oneida had become good friends with the British settlers. The Indians did not know what to do or who to believe when some of those settlers began to speak poorly about Great Britain. Samuel Kirkland had always told the Iroquois to honor the monarch of Great Britain. Now he was telling them that the king was an evil man not to be trusted.

At first the Iroquois Confederacy was reluctant to side with the American colonists because of the "Chain of Friendship" they had made with the English a hundred years earlier. Since the **League**, or Confederacy, felt it was important to maintain that friendship, it preferred to remain neutral during the war. The League hoped that the colonists would be able to settle their fight with Great Britain without involving the Indians.

Proclamation of Neutrality

The Oneida sent a **Proclamation of Neutrality** to the Americans from the Six Nations. It stated that under no circumstances would they participate in the quarrel. The Oneida said it was up to the American colonists to settle their own disputes. Because fighting had begun, the proclamation had no effect, and it became clear that the League could not remain neutral. After many **council** meetings, the Six Nations finally resolved the issue. They followed the advice of a Mohawk chief named Joseph Brant. He suggested

Chief Joseph Brant said each Iroquois nation should choose who to support during the American Revolution.

A tall monument, or obelisk, helps keep alive the memory of the 1777 Battle of Oriskany. In that bloody conflict, Oneida warriors fought with American soldiers against British forces and won the day.

that each nation decide for itself what course to take in the war. With the encouragement of Samuel Kirkland and Shenandoah, the Oneida and the Tuscarora sided with the colonists. The other Iroquois nations supported the British.

Shenandoah was the strongest voice among the Oneidas who gave support to the Americans. He prevented a massacre at German Flats, New York, when he warned the Americans of an attack by the British. Oneida warriors were among the best scouts in the colonial Army. At the battle of Oriskany in 1777, the American General Nicholas Herkimer marched his four companies along with Oneida warriors into an ambush against Colonel Barry St. Leger and his troops. Oneidas fought in the forefront of this battle the whole day with great skill and bravery—a battle considered by many to be among the bloodiest of the war.

Many times Oneidas came to the defense of the colonists. One legend even has it that Oneidas may have saved the life of the Marquis de Lafayette, the highest-ranking French army officer and close friend and aide to General George Washington. What certainly is true is that Oneidas traveled on a long overland journey in winter to bring as many as several hundred bags of corn to General Washington and his troops at Valley Forge, after Washington's own countrymen had failed to bring them supplies. And Oneidas saved the lives of many sick and wounded soldiers through their knowledge of herbs and the healing arts. General George Washington personally commended one Oneida for her outstanding help. She was Polly Cooper, who had helped his soldiers and taught them how to make medicine from various plants. Washington gave her a shawl as a token of his gratitude.

On April 9, 1779, the Continental Congress recognized the nation's appreciation for military support by granting commissions (certificates of military rank) to Oneida soldiers. Four Oneidas were made captains, and eight were appointed as lieutenants. In battle, Oneidas upheld their tradition of decency. Oneida warriors served honorably, and none of them harmed any women, children, or elderly.

Support Backfires

In 1778 Joseph Brant, with a force of Mohawk and other Iroquois, as well as British soldiers, attacked American forces and their Oneida and Tuscarora allies. This was in violation of the Great Law of the Confederacy, which forbade its members from making war against each other. British troops and Brant's warriors swept through parts of Pennsylvania and New York, including Oneida territory, leaving a path of destruction. The next year George Washington sent General John Sullivan on a mission of "total destruction and devastation" to repay the hostile Iroquois. He did so, and the attacks were merciless, destroying some 40 villages and huge supplies of corn. So awful were the results that Iroquois still refer to the President of the United States by a name that means "destroyer of villages."

In the 1783 **Treaty** of Paris, which ended the war, no provisions were made for the members of the Six Nations. Once the war was over, white settlers began to move west through Six Nations territory. The U.S. government, New York State government, as well as land companies, and other speculators all put pressure on the Indians, Oneidas included, to give up their lands. After the war, the Oneidas established separate communities depending on which side, the Americans or the British, they had supported. That division also made it easier for the state of New York to find individual Oneidas to sell their land in illegal negotiations. The Iroquois homeland was ruined, and the confederacy broke apart.

It was a bitter time, made even more bitter because the United States had taken many Iroquois ideas about government and incorporated them into the constitution of the new nation. None of those noble ideas helped the

Lakwaho McLester, the coauthor's grandson, holds a replica of the Washington Covenant Belt. During George Washington's presidency, the original belt represented a covenant of peace between the thirteen original states and the six Iroquois nations.

Iroquois, including the Oneida. They faced desperate times. Some of the nations fled, many north to Canada, with some Oneidas among them. (A group of Oneida chiefs moved to a settlement near Brantford, which today is called Six Nations. It is located in Ontario, 40 miles [64 km] west of Niagara Falls.) The hardships of the Oneida grew greater as their homeland became smaller. It shrank from some 6 million acres (2.4 million ha) to fewer than 1,000 acres (400 ha).

As the pressure on Oneidas to sell their land increased, it became clear to them that their only chance of survival was to move. One group moved to the Green Bay, Wisconsin, area,

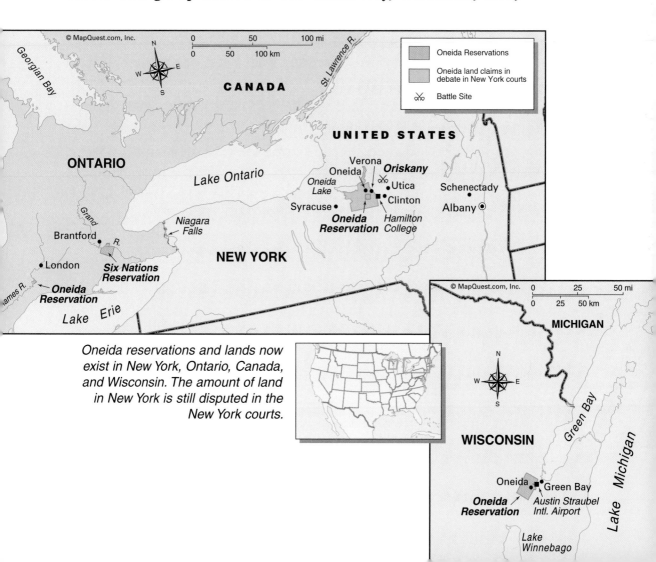

Oneida reservations and lands now exist in New York, Ontario, Canada, and Wisconsin. The amount of land in New York is still disputed in the New York courts.

and the other group moved to Canada. This left fewer than 200 Oneidas living on less than 1,200 acres (485 ha) in New York.

Those who remained in the United States were forced to live on **reservations**. The Oneida suffered along with the other nations. Sadly, the Americans whom they supported pushed them away from their territory. All the earlier promises the Americans had given the Oneida for protection, land, and goodwill were forgotten. The Oneida were scattered to the winds, and their descendants still live today in three different regions—Canada, Wisconsin, and New York.

As for Shenandoah, he had fought alongside people he thought were friends of the Oneida, only to see their homeland taken away at every turn. He felt that the Oneida had become mice before the cat when dealing with the white man. Kirkland was in an awkward position, because he was under pressure to urge the Oneida out of their territory, and that was something he had serious doubts about. In the end he received a large land grant. Kirkland died in 1808, and Shenandoah died in 1816, having passed the age of 100. The two men were buried next to each other at Hamilton College in Clinton, New York. The college was originally founded as Hamilton-Oneida Academy to bring education to the Oneida.

Leaving the Homeland

In the 1820s an Episcopalian missionary, Eleazer Williams, visited the Oneida. He was part Mohawk, and he could speak the Oneida language. This made it easier for Williams to convert Oneidas to Christianity. He also worked with some powerful people in Washington, D.C., and New York on a plan to move not only the Oneida—but all the members of the Six Nations—out of New York State.

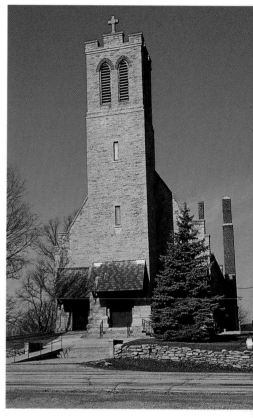

The Holy Apostles Episcopal Church on the Oneida Reservation in Wisconsin is a reminder of the missionary work of Eleazer Williams in the 1820s. About 70 percent of Wisconsin's Oneidas are still members of the church.

Williams hoped to organize a new Six Nations in the West, where he would be the leader. Under great pressure, approximately 650 Oneidas moved to land near present-day Green Bay, Wisconsin, between 1822 and 1838. They had negotiated with the Menominee and Ho-Chunk Indians for 65,000 acres (26,305 ha). The Oneida began to change from a hunting and gathering society to farming as a means of livelihood. The 65,000 acres were held in common by all members of the nation. Each member used only the amount of land that his or her family could farm. This left many acres remaining as forest.

In 1840 another group of Oneidas left the homeland in New York State and moved to Ontario, Canada. The party numbered 436, and they purchased 5,000 acres (2,024 ha) to live on. This left fewer than 200 Oneidas remaining in New York to live on about 1,400 acres (566 ha). The land in New York continued to be lost until 1920, when a court case ruled in favor of the Oneidas. What was their prize? A pitiful 32 acres (13 ha) to call their own. The Oneida have always claimed that their land was taken illegally, and they are still in the courts of New York trying to get it back—after nearly 200 years.

In 1887 Congress passed the **General Allotment Act**. This was supposed to help the Indians become better farmers, because now each would get his or her own piece of land and

"Keeper of the Oneida Language," and World War II veteran, Amos Christjohn, at left, coauthor Gordon McLester, center, and Lloyd Powless confer at a 1989 powwow held in Stuggart, Germany.

do with it what he or she wished, including selling it. Now the nation no longer held in common the 65,000 acres of land.

Standing at the Oneidas' doors were people who wanted their land again. It was clear that the Oneida were not ready for the effects of the General Allotment Act. By the 1930s nearly all the land had passed out of Oneida hands. Once again they had lost almost all of their lands!

In 1934 Congress passed the **Indian Reorganization Act**. This act was to help landless Indians get some land back and set up a different type of tribal government. The Oneida got 2,000 acres (810 ha) back, but most of it was swamp and not suitable for farming. The economic depression came, and there was no work. Then World War II started. Again, just as they had done in the Revolutionary War, the War of 1812, the Civil War, and in World War I, Oneidas stepped forward to fight. In fact, there may be no group in American society that has sent a greater percentage of its men to fight in American wars than the Oneida. Also during World War II, many Oneidas went to cities to work in defense plants, building equipment to fight the war.

Way of Life

Villages

Oneida villages provided homes for as many as 2,000 people. They were usually built along streams or lakes on a flat piece of land at the top of a steep hill. For protection from enemies, Oneidas surrounded each village with palisades, or walls of logs, 20 feet (6 m) high. The only entry into the fortresses was through two doorways at opposite ends of the village. These doorways were only about 3 feet (1 m) wide, so they could be blocked easily if the villagers were under attack.

Longhouses

The Oneida lived in longhouses. Each one was about 18 feet (5.5 m) wide and 18 feet high and varied in length from 40 to 300 feet (12 to 90 m), depending on the number of families living in it.

Longhouses were made from elm trees. First, bark was peeled from the trees, laid flat in stacks to dry, and weighed down with stones to prevent the bark from warping. Then thick branches were dug into the earth to frame the house. Next, the branches were bent to form arches for the roof. These were tied together with green saplings (cut young trees). Finally the bark was secured to the sides and top to create walls and a roof. The only doors were set at the far ends of each longhouse.

A photograph of a reconstructed longhouse shows the wood frame, bark siding, smoke holes in the roof, and doorways at each end of the building.

A longhouse with six smoke holes could have been home to 12 families. Some houses were three times larger.

An aisle containing fire pits ran down the center of the longhouse. Above each fire pit, a hole in the roof let smoke escape. Each cooking **hearth** was used by two families that lived across the aisle from each other. All families living in a longhouse were related to each other through the wives or mothers. As more families joined a longhouse, new sections were added. Some longhouses had as many as 24 fire pits and were very long indeed.

Each Oneida family had its own compartment about 20 feet (6 m) long. Family members sat and slept on low-lying platforms that were built along three sides of the compartment. The side facing the aisle and fire pit was open. Above the platforms shelves held clothes, weapons, baskets, and household goods. The families' bunks were covered with cornhusks to make the beds softer. Animal furs were used for blankets. Tribal leaders met in longhouses to conduct business. Some longhouses were specifically built to be the center of tribal ceremonial life.

Agriculture and Food

The Oneida became primarily a farming people, although the men fished and hunted deer, rabbits, and other animals. Women tended nearby garden plots, where they grew corn, beans, and squash. The Oneida called those crops the "**three** sisters." The "three sisters" was also a symbolic term, which stood for women, the family, and the continuity of Oneida society.

Europeans who came to live among the Oneida and other Iroquois nations introduced them to new foods. These included fruits such as apples, peaches, pears, and cherries, as well as chicken, pigs, and other meats. Food not cooked and eaten immediately was stored in pits dug into the ground. Fruits and vegetables were placed in baskets, and meats were wrapped in deerskin before they were stored.

The "three sisters" of planted crops: corn, squash and beans, had some brothers: pumpkins and a root crop like carrots.

To make cornbread, one has to pound the corn into meal, as shown here on the Six Nations Reserve in Canada.

Arts and Crafts

The Oneida excelled at wood carving and basket making. Although women were the primary basket makers, some men also became expert at the craft. A variety of materials were used to make baskets, including elm bark, cornhusks, cattails, sweet grass, and black ash. Black ash was used to make storage and utility baskets. Sweet grass was used only for coiled baskets. To make this type of basket, grass was twisted and then made into layered coils. It is a technique similar to that used in making clay pots. Cornhusks and cattails were used to make sandals, mats, and snowshoes.

Perhaps about 1900, a young woman wove a basket next to a birch bark canoe (above).

This basket (right) was made from sweet grass coiled tightly, topped by a carving of a turtle on the lid.

A pair of shoes made from decorated cornhusks (left) were used on special occasions.

Some of the wood carving was done to make medicine masks, which are also known as "false face masks." Each design came from the vision of the carver, so no two masks were identical. The masks were made from a live basswood tree, sometimes decorated with brass tacks and horsehair. These masks were used to help prevent or cure illnesses in ceremonies that some Oneidas still celebrate today.

Oneidas are also famous for their "dream catchers" made of strips of wood and rawhide and decorated with shells and feathers. A long time ago, the Oneida adopted the making of the dream catcher from the Ojibwa. During the night the dream catcher, which was hung near the bed, would catch your dreams, good or bad. Bad dreams would be caught in the webbing of the dream catcher and held there until dawn. Then the rays from the sun would chase them away. The good dreams would make their way to the hole in the center of the dream catcher. They would then move down to the feathers hanging at the bottom where the good dreams could be saved for another night. With a dream catcher nearby, children need not be afraid of having bad dreams. Dream catchers today are made of almost anything you can think of.

Oneidas also made faceless cornhusk dolls. It is said that the Creator once made a doll out of cornhusks, and the doll thought she was better than everyone else. Because it is wrong to think that way, the Creator removed her face. To remind their children of that lesson, Oneidas do not put faces on their cornhusk dolls.

Cornhusk dolls usually did not have faces painted on them. Some were plain (left), and some were decorated in bright colors (right).

After Europeans arrived and showed them how, Oneidas began making silver jewelry. They became interested in metalworking after receiving silver medals and coins as gifts from the French and the Dutch. Soon the Oneida began trading furs for metal tools as well as pieces of silver to make their own finger rings, earrings, and other pieces of jewelry. Oneida jewelers were especially noted for their distinctive circular brooches (pins) decorated with arches and crosses.

Clothing

Before Europeans arrived, Oneida clothing was made from tanned deerskins. Seventeen skins were needed each year to clothe a family of five. Women made nearly all the clothing. When trade with the Europeans began in the 1600s, broadcloth soon replaced deer hides. Men wore moccasins, shirts, and leggings. They also wore aprons with neck openings that went over the top part of their body from front to back. Women wore moccasins, leggings from the knees down, skirts, and long blouses. Traditional clothes are still worn for special occasions such as Oneida powwows, weddings, and other ceremonies held throughout the year.

Some of coauthor McLester's family (left) gather together, including his daughter-in-law Caterina, and her children Lakwaho and Yuntle of the Wolf Clan, and daughter Jennifer, with children Zack, Mark, and Olivia of the Turtle Clan, and her husband Don.

Craig Marvin (right), a young Mohawk dancer, performs in traditional dress at the Native American Dance and Music Festival.

Lacrosse

The sport of lacrosse started with the Iroquois, who played it long before Europeans arrived. The sticks were made originally of hickory wood, and the pockets to cradle the ball were made from rawhide. (The wooden balls used then were larger than the rubber balls now used.)

Alf Jacques, an Onondaga, makes traditional wood lacrosse sticks, long used by Oneidas and other Iroquois peoples in the fast-paced game now popular as a school and college sport.

Europeans were amazed and delighted by the game, which featured hundreds of players racing across a playing field as much as a mile long. In fact, it was a French missionary who named the game. He thought the sticks used to move the ball around the field resembled a bishop's staff, so he called the game *la crosse*, which means "the crook." Today Iroquois teams compete in lacrosse tournaments all over the world. Oneidas play lacrosse with other Indian communities and local colleges, and lacrosse is part of the Midwinter **Ceremony**.

Spiritual Life

Ceremonies

Although many Oneidas have adopted and follow the Christian faith, there are other Oneidas that still hold to the Traditional beliefs. Just as the Christian Oneidas attend church on Sunday, the Traditional Oneidas attend the Ceremonies that start with the changing of the seasons of Mother Earth.

Many Oneida ceremonies follow those changing cycles, and Oneidas believe they are related to the Earth. The Earth is their mother. The sun is their elder brother. The moon is their grandmother, and the thunder is their grandfather. Oneidas also believe that animals are their brothers and that plants are their sisters.

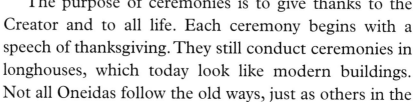

Mother Earth, drawn as an Oneida woman, cradles her precious offspring.

The purpose of ceremonies is to give thanks to the Creator and to all life. Each ceremony begins with a speech of thanksgiving. They still conduct ceremonies in longhouses, which today look like modern buildings. Not all Oneidas follow the old ways, just as others in the Six Nations have people that follow different ways. There is a longhouse at each of the three Oneida communities that are

This log longhouse in Wisconsin follows the traditional patterns, but includes such contemporary features as a solar panel and three windows, rather than smoke holes, that admit light.

A French engraving from the 1730s shows Iroquois women, perhaps Oneidas, preparing maple syrup, while other women work at planting the fields beyond. Farming has changed greatly, but making maple syrup is just about the same as it was nearly 400 years ago.

used for the ceremonies throughout the year. The longhouse is also used for weddings and funerals much the same way that Christian churches are.

Many ceremonies are held during the year. First is the Midwinter Ceremony. It celebrates the beginning of the new year and the waking of Mother Earth, who has been sleeping through the cold winter. Next is the Maple Ceremony. It takes place in either February or March, depending on when the sap starts to flow in the sugar maple trees. Maple trees are given thanks for fulfilling their job of providing sap to make syrup as the Creator requested.

The Seed (or Planting) Ceremony starts the annual cycle of the crops. Thanks are given to the Creator for providing the seeds to feed families and to the seeds for growing. When the first thunder or rainstorms of the season arrive, the Thunder

Ceremony follows. The Strawberry Ceremony is especially important. Because the strawberry is the first plant to grow, it is considered a useful medicine as well as sacred. For that reason strawberries are used in a sacred ceremonial drink. Oneidas believe that strawberries will travel into the next world with someone who has died.

Rattles are an important part of ceremonies, because they help keep the tempo of songs and dances. Originally Oneidas made rattles from gourds and turtle shells. Now many are made from cow horns. Turtle rattles have special meaning, for the Oneidas believe that the Mother Earth rests on a turtle's back (see the Creation Story, p. 5). The 13 spaces on the turtle's shell represent the 13 moons in the Oneidas' seasonal system.

Ceremonial rattles (far left) are now often made of cow horns.

Ready for a ceremonial dance (left), Lakwaho McLester is dressed in traditional Oneida costume and carries a horn rattle.

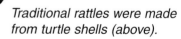

Traditional rattles were made from turtle shells (above).

Family Life

Oneida society is based on a system of **clans**. There are many stories describing how clans came to be, but it is generally believed they were established before the Iroquois Confederacy agreed to the **Great Law of Peace**. This is one version of the clan story:

The Clan Story

Many years ago in the distant past, the people got along with each other. Everyone, including first and second cousins, were considered to be part of each family. As the population grew, people began to argue and to fight with one another. Everyone was unhappy. Hoping to restore respect and peace among the people, the elders called a meeting to discuss the situation. After much discussion, a young man stepped forward. He urged the people to follow the example provided by animals in nature, such as birds, and divide themselves into groups called clans. The idea so impressed the elders that they named the young man He Who Has Great Ideas.

He Who Has Great Ideas suggested that the people pack their belongings and prepare to travel. The next morning they followed him to a nearby river. While everyone watched, he grabbed a long vine hanging from a tree and swung himself across the river. After landing on the other side, he told them to follow him, but only half were able to make it across. He Who Has Great Ideas then told the women of each family to pay close attention to anything unusual they might see in the morning.

The next day, when an elderly woman went to fetch water down by the river, she heard a noise and looked up to see a

deer. Upon telling He Who Has Great Ideas about the deer, he told her that the deer would be the clan symbol for her and all her offspring forever. This meant that the clans would be passed down from the mothers to their children, making Iroquois society **matrilineal**.

This story was repeated several times on both sides of the river. On one side were seen a deer, a bear, a snipe (a slender-billed bird), and an eel. On the other side of the river were seen a wolf, a beaver, a turtle, and a hawk. Each of the creatures symbolized a clan. The four clans on each side of the river formed a group called a **moiety**. From that time on, whenever an Iroquois boy and girl wanted to get married, they had to make certain that they belonged to different moieties.

Oneida Clans

The Oneida, along with other members of the Six Nations, used their clan systems to determine everyone's family. Some nations had more clans than other nations. The Oneidas and the Mohawk each have three clans. They are Wolf, Bear, and Turtle. Each of the three Oneida clans had three chiefs, or sachems. (The word "sachem" comes from the name of a pole used to support a longhouse.) This gave the Oneidas nine chiefs that would represent them at the Grand Council of the Six Nations.

The flag of the "Oneida Nation of Wisconsin" shows traditional elements such as the Tree of Peace and the three clans—Wolf, Bear, and Turtle.

Clan mothers have the responsibility of watching over and directing members of their clan. In addition, the clan mothers are responsible for the selection of the chiefs of their clans. They also have the authority to remove those chiefs if they don't do the things that are best for the people. Other members of the Six Nations that had similar clans were looked upon as close family relations.

The women were called the keepers of the land, and they cared for the work in the fields, the upkeep of the village, as well as raised and educated the children. The men's jobs were hunting, fishing, meeting in council, or fighting in war.

Clan Characteristics

The people in each clan tend to have distinct characteristics. For example, it is said that people in the Turtle clan tend to be shy and easygoing. They do not like to be surprised or rushed into doing anything. In a sense, they are like real turtles who withdraw into their shells if suddenly startled. Members of the Turtle clan are cordial but cautious with each new person they meet. It takes time to become close friends with a member of the Turtle clan.

Members of the Bear clan can also be quiet and shy. But, like real bears, they can become quite fierce if angered in any way. They also have an incredible knowledge of medicines. They know which plants and herbs can cure various ailments, and

Robert Bennett (left) of the Turtle Clan served as Commissioner of the Bureau of Indian Affairs. Olivia Webster (right), granddaughter of the coauthor, also of the Turtle Clan, is dressed in a "buckskin" dress at a powwow.

they also know the power of the sacred medicines. Members of the Bear clan are known as healers.

Members of the Wolf clan tend to be aggressive, much like real wolves. They are not as sensitive to the feelings of others as are members of the Turtle and Bear clans. They enjoy getting into arguments, and they seem to have feuds just for the sake of having them. The people in the Wolf clan are hard workers who will rally and unite if any harm comes to a clan member.

The Role of Women

Women have an important role in the clans. Because they live in a matrilineal society, Oneida women own their homes and the belongings in the homes. Like Mother Earth, they nurture people from birth until death.

Women are responsible for raising children, teaching them to be leaders, and preparing them to be thoughtful and upstanding citizens in society. Elders share this responsibility by teaching children about their ancestors and their heritage.

The three oldest women in each clan are the most important. Because they have acquired a great deal of wisdom and have experienced so much in their long lives, the three women are called clan mothers. It is the clan mothers who select the nine chiefs or sachems who govern the nation.

Holding horn rattles, Caterina and Yuntle McLester sing "social songs," which are sung just for fun during a break from a traditional ceremony.

Tribal Government

The U.S. Political System and the Iroquois Confederacy

The Iroquois Confederacy worked so well that the founding fathers of the United States are said to have considered aspects of it in developing the plan for linking the thirteen colonies into a united country. Benjamin Franklin, for one, admired the Iroquois form of government.

The similarities are striking. For example, the Onondaga were the fire keepers of the Grand Council. Their role was like that of the President of the United States, who heads the executive branch. The Iroquois sachems who attended the Grand Council were divided into two parts like the legislative branch of the U.S. government. The Elder Brothers, the Mohawk and the Seneca, formed the upper house of the Grand Council. That was equivalent to the U.S. Senate. The Younger Brothers, the Oneida and Cayuga, were very much like the House of Representatives. The Great Law of Peace is like the Constitution of the United States. (The adopted Tuscarora were members of the Confederacy but had no say or chiefs on the council.)

A delegation of Iroquois, including Oneida, visited Philadelphia in May 1776, just before the British colonists in America declared their independence. The Indians had planned to be neutral, but many were forced to choose one side or the other.

Contemporary Life

The Oneidas Today

In 1920 the Oneidas still living in New York State won a court case that recognized their ownership of 32 acres (13 ha) of the original Oneida homeland. Even so, it was not until the 1960s that federal programs began to bring Oneidas back home. Today they have increased the land base to more than 10,000 acres (4,050 ha). About 1,500 Oneidas live on or near the homeland in New York.

The Oneida Nation in New York has become successful. Many Oneida-owned businesses provide jobs and income for the people. These include Turning Stone Casino and Hotel, the Turning Stone RV Park and Convenience Store, and several service stations near Verona, New York. The 32 acres now support a pool, playground, pavilion (recreation place), lacrosse and softball field, a gym, a teen center, and a Council House and burial ground. The nation has also built a cultural center, health center, and a center for reestablishing the Oneida language.

Oneida girls work on a project that teaches them about their heritage at the Oneida Tribal School in Wisconsin.

New homes are being built in the village of White Pines. The Oneidas have also begun construction of a combined learning center for the elders and children to give the elders the opportunity to teach Oneida youngsters about their traditions.

In 1974 the Oneida Nation of Wisconsin started a bingo hall, and Oneida gaming facilities have continued to expand ever since. People from all over the United States now come to the Oneida Reservation near Green Bay to play bingo. They stay in Oneida Radisson Hotel, which houses a restaurant, gift shop, and conference center. It is conveniently located across from Green Bay's Austin Straubel Airport.

Other businesses, such as the Oneida Tobacco Industry, a canning facility, a large industrial park, and several Oneida One Stop service stations and convenience stores, are thriving. From profits made Oneidas have provided services for people of all ages in their community, such as the Oneida Senior Center, the Oneida Nursing Home, the Oneida Health Care Center and Pharmacy, and the Oneida Civic Center. Income also supports programs that treat people who suffer from drug and alcohol abuse and from domestic abuse. The money funds the Oneida Museum, the Oneida Community Library, the Oneida Transit Authority, and many other excellent services as well.

In 1979 Wisconsin Oneidas built and opened the Oneida Tribal School. Not only does it provide education in reading, writing, and arithmetic, but it also gives their children the opportunity to learn about their heritage, culture, and language. Of

Learning, tradition, and legend come together at the Oneida Tribal School in Wisconsin—built in the shape of the giant turtle.

An Iroquois man guides a steel girder while building a skyscraper in New York City.

great importance to the nation, the Oneida of Wisconsin have also managed to get back about 3,000 acres (1,214 ha) of the land they lost. They have accomplished this by buying property as it comes up for sale.

The Oneida of Canada still live in the region along the Thames River of Ontario, which they bought in 1840. Their numbers have increased to perhaps 3,000 to 5,000, and many follow traditional ways. Many also work in nearby towns and cities in such trades as construction. Among them are highly skilled iron workers who assemble "high steel," the frameworks for towering skyscrapers and bridges. Not only Oneidas, but other Iroquois workers have long been famous for their ability to set beams in place at dizzying heights. They do so where there is nothing but sky above them and a long, long way down to the ground.

Because of all these vigorous programs and renewed feelings of optimism, more and more Oneidas are returning to their homelands and revitalizing the splendid culture their ancestors once knew and celebrated. With time and patience they should succeed.

Oneida Indian Dean Doxtator begins his traditional dance in open competition at the Indian Village of the New York State Fair in Geddes, New York.

Oneida Prayer

(In Oneida)	(Sounds like)	(In English)
Tak wa nuh wehla tu	Dug way new he law do	We give you thanks
Yunkhinulha	Yunk key new lha	Our Mother
oh w^ts yake	Oh hoon jaw gay	On Earth.
Tsi Wa Sk wa,v^	Ge wa ska auh	You have given us
Kak wa oku	Gwak wa oh goo	All the food
Aet wate kuni	A ed wade koon	For us to eat.
Tani	Donni	That's all.

Oneida Recipes

Maple Sugar Cookies

Adult supervision is required.

1 cup maple syrup
$\frac{1}{2}$ cup hot water
$\frac{1}{2}$ cup butter
$2\frac{1}{2}$ cups flour
2 teaspoons baking powder
$\frac{1}{2}$ teaspoon cinnamon
$\frac{1}{2}$ teaspoon ginger
$\frac{1}{2}$ teaspoon ground cloves

Yummy maple sugar cookies

Preheat oven to 325° F.
Mix maple syrup, hot water, and butter. Then mix dry ingredients and add. Mix all together well. Drop teaspoonfuls of batter on a cookie sheet and bake for 10 to 15 minutes. Sprinkle with powdered sugar.

Baked Walleye

Adult supervision is required.

4 walleye fillets
4 teaspoons melted butter
4 teaspoons lemon juice
$\frac{1}{4}$ teaspoon salt

Preheat oven to 350° F.
Put walleye fillets side-by-side in a jelly roll pan. Add enough water to just cover the bottom of the pan. Brush each fillet with melted butter and lemon juice. Sprinkle lightly with salt. Bake 10 to 20 minutes until fish is milky white, basting from time to time with butter and lemon juice.

Oneida Game

Lacrosse

Lacrosse is the best known and most popular game invented by Iroquois people. Today it resembles a cross between hockey, soccer, and Irish hurling. It is played with curved sticks with mesh pockets that are used to scoop, carry, and pass a small, hard ball. Each team has one goalie defending a net and several players who specialize in offense or defense. The game requires speed, constant running, ball handling, passing, and teamwork.

Modern lacrosse is played by both men's and women's teams, usually at high school and college levels. It is particularly popular among Iroquois people and in Eastern Canada and the United States, although its popularity is spreading across North America and even in Europe.

Modern lacrosse adds helmets, pads, and gloves for protection. Most lacrosse sticks are now made out of fiberglass. But the spirit of the game is the same as in ancient days.

Oneida Chronology

A.D. 900–1150	The Iroquois spread across northeastern North America.
1400	The classic longhouse design is established.
Before 1500	The Iroquois Confederacy is formed.
1535	Jacques Cartier explores the St. Lawrence River.
1600s [or before]	Clothes are made from deer hides.
1600s	The Dutch make contact with the Oneida.
1609	Samuel de Champlain meets and communicates with the Iroquois.
1634	A smallpox epidemic rages through the nations.
1706	Shenandoah is born.
1766	Samuel Kirkland arrives to establish a mission among the Oneidas and Tuscaroras.
1779	Joseph Brant campaigns with other nations and the British to fight the Oneidas and Tuscaroras.
1790	The Trade and Intercourse Act is passed.
1822	The Oneida begin to move to Wisconsin.
1848	Only 200 Oneidas remain in New York. Wisconsin becomes a state.
1887	The General Allotment (or Dawes) Act of 1887 is passed.
1924	The U.S. government permits Oneidas to become U.S. citizens, but the New York Oneidas refuse.
1934	The Indian Reorganization Act of 1934 is established.
1960	The Oneidas move back onto their land, which now consists of only 32 acres (12 ha).
1974	The Oneida Bingo Hall in Wisconsin opens.
1979	The Oneida Tribal School opens in Wisconsin.
1985	The Oneida Bingo Hall in New York opens.
1986	The Oneida Radisson Hotel opens in Wisconsin.
1990s	Turning Stone Casino in New York and many other establishments in New York and Wisconsin are opened.

Glossary

Ceremony A formal sacred act.

Clan A group of related families descended from a common ancestor.

Clan mothers The three eldest women in a clan.

Council A group of people that come together to hold meetings that concern the different clans.

General Allotment Act of 1887 A law establishing a policy to remove Native Americans from the land they inhabited and divide their land into allotments.

Grand Council Members from all Six Nations who come together to discuss issues that affect the general interest.

Great Law of Peace, The A set of laws that describes how the Iroquois Confederacy should live.

Great Tree, The The tree through which the Sky People sustained life.

Hearth A small hole dug out from the earth that was used to contain fires.

Indian Reorganization Act of 1934 This act helped reestablish the Oneidas in Wisconsin economically.

Iroquois Confederacy, or Haudenosaunee (HO-de-NO-sah-nee) Means "people of the longhouse." The Confederacy is an alliance of six Indian nations—the Oneida, the Cayuga, the Seneca, the Onondaga, the Mohawk, and the Tuscarora.

League A group of people joined together for a common purpose.

Legend A story that has been passed down from generation to generation.

Longhouse The home in which the people resided. It also refers to the practice of traditional ways and ceremonies.

Matrilineal Descent of family through the mother.

Moiety Two equal parts. In anthropology, it means the primary subdivisions in a nation.

Nation A community of people who share a common language and culture.

Peacemaker, The A holy man who speaks the word of peace.

Proclamation of Neutrality An announcement from the Iroquois saying they would not participate in the fight between the colonists and the British in the Revolutionary War.

Reservation Public land set aside for a specific use.

Sachem (SAY-chem) A chief or representative. It literally means a pole used for support in a longhouse.

Three Sisters, The Corn, beans, and squash. They are the sustainers of life for the Iroquois and are a gift from the Creator.

Treaty An agreement made between two or more nations.

Tree of Peace, The Symbolizes the end to fighting among the Iroquois nations.

Further Reading

Bierhorst, John, edited by. *The Naked Bear—Folktales of the Iroquois*. New York: William Morrow and Company, 1987.

Bruchac, Joseph. *The Boy Who Lived with the Bears and Other Iroquois Stories*. New York: HarperCollins, 1995.

De Coteau Orie, Sandra. *Did You Hear Wind Sing Your Name? An Oneida Song of Spring*. New York: Walker and Company, 1995.

Duvall, Jill. *The Oneidas*. Chicago: Children's Press, 1991.

Hoyt-Goldsmith, Diane. *Lacrosse: The National Game of the Iroquois*. New York: Holiday House, 1998.

Viola, Herman J. *North American Indians: An Introduction to the Lives of America's Native Peoples, From the Inuit of the Arctic to the Zuni of the Southwest*. New York: Crown Publishers, 1996.

Sources

Doherty, Craig A., and Katherine M. *The Iroquois*. New York: Franklin Watts, 1991.

Graymont, Barbara. *The Iroquois*. New York: Chelsea House Publishers, 1988.

Hauptman, Laurence M., and Gordon McLester, III, eds. *The Oneida Journey from Wisconsin to New York 1784–1860*. Madison, WI: The University of Wisconsin Press, 1999.

Porter, Tom. *Clanology: Clan Systems of the Iroquois*. Cornwall, Ontario: North American Indian Travelling College Teachings, 1993–1994.

Realm of the Iroquois. Alexandria, VA: Time-Life Books, 1993.

Wilbur M.D., Keith C. *The Woodland Indians: An Illustrated Account of the Lifestyles of America's First Inhabitants*. Broomall, PA: Chelsea House Publishers, 1995.

Index

Numbers in italics indicate illustration or map.

48